The Library of Cells™

Cell Regulation

Understanding How Cell Functions, Growth, and Division Are Regulated

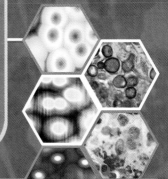

Lois Sakany

The Rosen Publishing Group, Inc., New York

Published in 2005 by The Rosen Publishing Group, Inc.
29 East 21st Street, New York, NY 10010

Copyright © 2005 by The Rosen Publishing Group, Inc.

First Edition

Library of Congress Cataloging-in-Publication Data

Sakany, Lois.
Cell regulation: understanding how cell functions, growth,
and division are regulated/by Lois Sakany.—1st ed.
    p. cm.—(The library of cells)
Includes bibliographical references and index.
ISBN 1-4042-0321-4 (library binding)
1. Cellular control mechanisms—Juvenile literature.
I. Title. II. Series.
QH604.S25 2005
571.6—dc22

                                        2004018821

Manufactured in the United States of America

On the cover: This light micrograph shows a section of
a green leaf. Each cell contains several round, green
vesicles called chloroplasts. These organelles contain the
green pigment chlorophyll and are found in the cells of
all green plants.

Contents

Introduction

Nowadays, electron micrographs and drawings of cells, which both illustrate cell parts, are commonplace. However, when we look at cell images on either the page of a book or a computer screen, there is one key aspect that is missing: living cells are not static.

Because cells are alive, they are constantly in motion inside our bodies. In order to properly function, cells may, at various stages, change, grow, develop, or divide.

In order to understand how a cell regulates its most essential functions, it's important to know the basics of cell structure. In 1839, Theodor Schwann proposed the cell theory. Today, it remains a cornerstone of biology. Schwann proposed that all living things are composed of one or more cells; that all cells result from cells either through cell division or through the joining together of sex cells; that every cell is self-contained and partially self-sufficient; and that cells are the elementary unit of life.

Chapter One

Movement and Function

All cells fall into two categories; they are either prokaryotic cells or eukaryotic cells. Prokaryotic cells are simple cells such as single-celled bacteria that cause infections and other types of illness. Prokaryotic cells do not have a true nucleus.

More complex cells, which have more distinct and specialized organelles (the membrane-bound "little organs" inside the cell) are called eukaryotic cells. Eukaryotic cells make up organisms ranging in size from a single-celled paramecium to complex plants and animals composed of trillions of cells.

A complex organism contains hundreds of types of cells, each performing a different function. There are absorptive cells, which take in food and building materials and secretory cells whose function is to produce and move particles out of the cell. There are also sensory cells, which emit electrical signals. Those electrical signals are picked up by nerve cells, or neurons, which transmit the signals to muscle cells. In order to carry on life, higher organisms also have sex cells, which are designed to join with sex cells

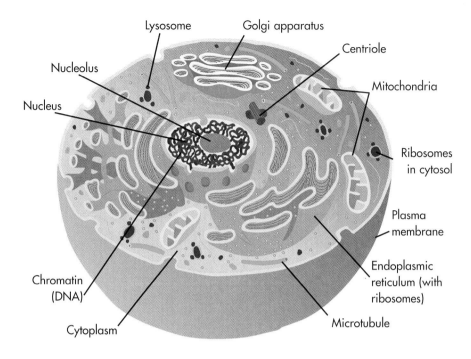

This illustration of a eukaryotic cell shows its organelles surrounded by a semipermeable plasma membrane. All animal cells, such as this one, include a nucleus, where DNA is contained; a nucleolus, the interior of the nucleus; and other organelles suspended in the jellylike cytoplasm. Other organelles pictured are the cell's mitochondria, endoplasmic reticulum, Golgi apparatus, lysosomes, ribosomes, microtubules, and centrioles.

from another organism to produce a genetically unique and new life-form.

However, whatever their function, all eukaryotic cells share similar structures that figure largely in how cell functions are regulated.

The Nucleus

The nucleus, or command center, is the most visible cell organelle. It is the main force in regulation of cell activity. Located near the center of the cell, it contains DNA (deoxyribonucleic acid), which, when

This bacterial cell is prokaryotic, which means that it lacks a true nucleus. Nuclear matter instead floats freely in the cell's interior cytoplasm along with its ribosomes. As in all cells, it is protected by an exterior plasma membrane. A single flagellum provides it with momentum.

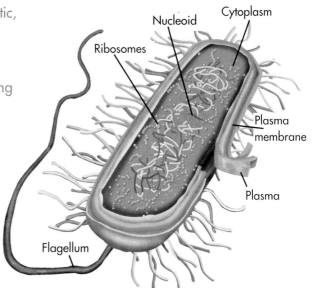

Cytoplasm

Nucleoid

Ribosomes

Plasma membrane

Plasma

Flagellum

combined with a specific form of protein, makes up the cell's chromosomes. Each organism has a set number of chromosomes. Chromosomes direct all the activities of the cell during its life span, including its growth and reproduction. During cell division, the chromosomes are responsible for passing on the traits of the cell to new cells.

Cell Membrane

One of the most important organs involved in cell regulation is the cell membrane. It has several regulatory roles, which include enclosing and protecting the cell. The cell membrane also acts as a gateway, designed to control what comes into and out of the cell. Think of the cell membrane as a wall surrounding a large factory. The wall is designed to control what comes into and out of the factory. In keeping with this example, there are entry points, or gateways, which are usually manned by someone who regulates who can enter or leave the factory. A cell membrane works in much the same way. A similar protective, semipermeable layer surrounds each organelle.

In comparing plant and animal cells, one of the major differences in their composition is the construction of the cell membrane. Unlike animal cells,

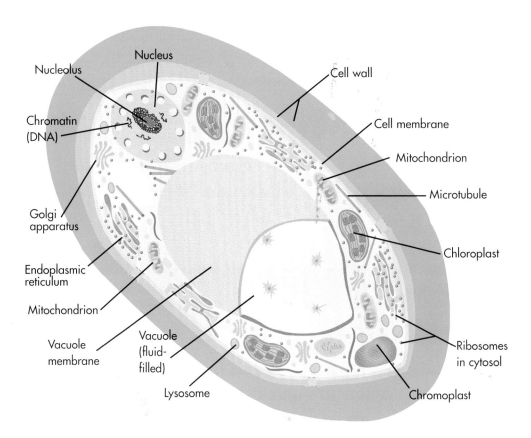

Plant cells contain organelles similar to those in eukaryotic animal cells, such as a nucleus, Golgi apparatus, mitochondria, and endoplasmic reticulum. What distinguishes plant cells from animal cells is their sturdy outer cell wall and green chromoplasts or chloroplasts, the large organelles that trap sunlight during photosynthesis. This process is unique to all green plant cells and creates oxygen as a waste product.

plant cells are surrounded by an outer cell wall. Strong and stiff, the cell wall is composed of a long chain of sugar molecules called cellulose. This rigid cell wall not only protects the cell but also enables it to grow tall and straight.

Endoplasmic Reticulum

The endoplasmic reticulum acts as the animal cell's transportation system. Like a funhouse maze, this organelle is made up of an elaborate path of tubular passageways. Some of the passageways lead from the nuclear membrane all the way to the cell membrane.

A variety of proteins and lipids (fats) essential to the cell's function are manufactured within the endoplasmic reticulum. The proteins and lipids are then either transported to other parts of the cell or out of the cell through its membrane. Much of the proteins and lipids manufactured in the endoplasmic reticulum go into making cell and organelle membranes.

The surface of the endoplasmic reticulum is dotted with RNA (ribonucleic acid), which produces various types of protein as needed by the cell. RNA receives its directions from the DNA in the nucleus. Once the protein is produced, it is sent away along the pathways of the endoplasmic reticulum.

Lysosomes and Vacuoles

Lysosomes are small, round organelles found throughout the cell. They contain digestive enzymes that can break down everything from large food molecules to invading bacteria and irreparable cell structures. When the lysosome breaks down food particles, the smaller molecules are passed on to the cell's "furnace," or mitochondria. In the mitochondria, these molecules are used to provide energy for the cell. There are also occasions when a cell might be given directions to self-destruct because, for whatever reason, the cell is no longer needed by the organism. In these cases, the lysosome will burst open, and its contents will spill into the cell and destroy it.

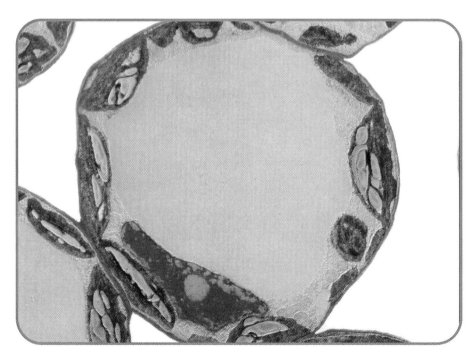

This colored transmission electron micrograph shows chloroplasts inside the leaf cells of a zinnia plant. The chloroplasts are situated on the edge of each cell. The starch granules (pink) inside them are a form of stored sugar. The cell's nucleus is colored red. The large center area (blue) is a fluid-filled vacuole.

Vacuoles are fluid-filled organelles that serve a variety of functions, including food and water storage. They are more commonly found in plant cells, in which they store water. Plant vacuoles take up and release water as needed by the plant. When the vacuoles are full, the plant looks lush and healthy because the fluid-filled vacuoles make the plant rigid and firm.

Mitochondria

Like a battery for a car, the rod-shaped mitochondria provide the cell with the energy it needs to

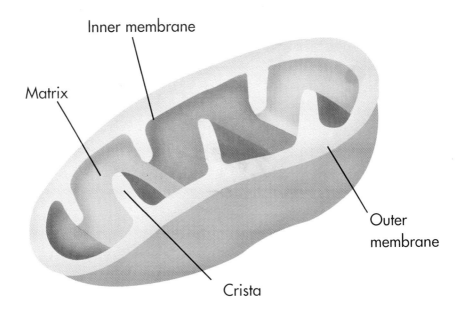

This mitochondrion (plural: mitochondria) is responsible for cellular respiration. Mitochondria are bound by double membranes, contain their own DNA inside the matrix (the projections into the matrix are called cristae), and reproduce by dividing in two.

manufacture proteins and lipids, break down food, maintain water balance, repair broken cell structures, and reproduce. Within the mitochondria, simple food substances such as sugar are further broken down into water and carbon dioxide gas. During this process, energy is released. This energy is stored in energy packets that the cell uses to do work. Mitochondria contain their own DNA and can multiply independently of the larger cell.

Chloroplasts

One major difference between plant and animal cells is that only plant cells contain chloroplasts. Irregularly shaped and found throughout the cell, chloroplasts contain a green pigment called chlorophyll. This pigment captures the energy of the Sun, which the cell then uses to make food. This process is called photosynthesis.

Chapter Two

Command Central

To examine the basics of cell regulation, it's important to start with the genes. This genetic material contains the blueprints for how the cell appears and functions. The genes are also responsible for which particles are able to cross the cell membrane, how energy is extracted from food particles, and when a cell reproduces.

Genes, specific chains of hereditary material, are made up of DNA. They are located along the cell's chromosomes, which are found within its nucleus. All cells contain a complete set of genes. However, only a small percentage of those genes are active at any given time.

Sending a Message

As powerful as genes are, however, they do not act independently. Genes are often motivated to act only after being switched "on" by other molecules in the cell. Rather than being independent, the cell's genes are not unlike the boss's office at a very busy factory. Activity and manufacturing take place throughout the building, and while not all of the decisions have to be made by consulting the boss, many do.

In order for cells to send and receive messages to their genes, there must be a system that responds to signals in the environment. These signals are actually a variety of molecules that have the ability to trigger an action. In science, the study of cell communication is called signal transduction.

The basic components of communication between two cells include a signaling cell and a receiving cell. A signaling cell produces a molecule that is detected by a receptor on another cell—the receiving cell. In this way, a signal received on the outside of the cell will be converted into a signal on the inside of the cell, which will then change a cell's behavior.

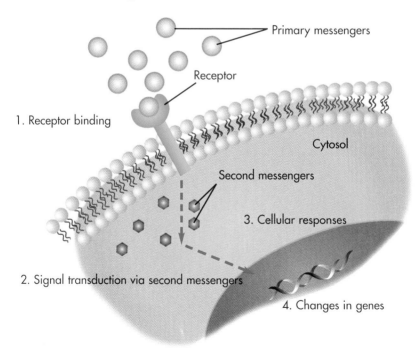

Primary messengers

Receptor

1. Receptor binding

Cytosol

Second messengers

3. Cellular responses

2. Signal transduction via second messengers

4. Changes in genes

This illustration shows the process of signal transduction, which is the conversion of a signal from one physical or chemical form to another. Inside a cell, signal transduction is the process by which a cell produces a response to an extracellular signal.

There are several types of communication signals. Some signals are contact dependent. They result after two cells come in direct contact with each other. Hormonal signaling (also called endocrinal signaling) occurs throughout the entire organism, usually triggered by the secretion of signals through the bloodstream. This type of communication can also occur on a more localized level. Finally, signaling can occur through nerve cells (also called neuronal signaling). Neuronal signaling sends electrical signals as directed by the organism's nervous system.

Endocrinal Signaling

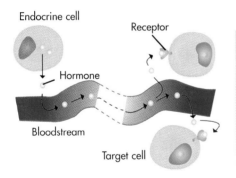

Contact-dependent Signaling

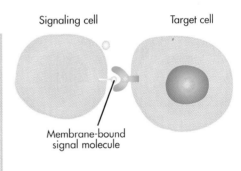

These diagrams show different kinds of cell signaling. Endocrinal and neuronal signaling are used by cells to communicate over long distances. Endocrinal signaling is accomplished when hormones are released, while neurons use chemicals called neurotransmitters to communicate. Contact-dependent signaling takes place between cells when information passes directly through their plasma membranes.

Neuronal Signaling

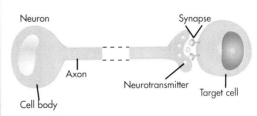

Manufacturing Protein

When the genes receive a request for a particular protein, rather than duplicate it within the nucleus, they allow their genetic sequence to be copied. This "copy" is created with the help of messenger RNA (mRNA). Once the information has been copied, the mRNA squeezes through the tiny pores of the nucleus and is picked up by one of the cell's many ribosomes.

Located within the endoplasmic reticulum, the ribosomes set to work creating the requested protein. This process is remarkably quick. In a single cell, for example, ribosomes manufacture an estimated 2,000 new protein molecules per second.

If the protein is destined for use within the cytoplasm, the cell's jellylike interior, the ribosome will manufacture it while drifting freely in the cell. If the protein has a more specialized destination—such as on the plasma membrane as a receptor—then the ribosome will manufacture the protein along the surface of the endoplasmic reticulum.

Once there, the endoplasmic reticulum will further modify the ribosome's protein into the appropriate shape. Again, depending on the protein, it may be changed again in the organelle known as the Golgi apparatus, the storage organelle for proteins and lipids. The protein is then sorted according to its type and final destination.

Gateway to the Cell

Much of the regulatory signaling that takes place in a cell occurs on either the membrane surrounding the cell or inside one of its organelles. Cell membranes are semipermeable membranes, that is, some molecules are able to pass through them but not all. This function enables the cell to maintain an environment inside the cell that is different from the environment outside the cell.

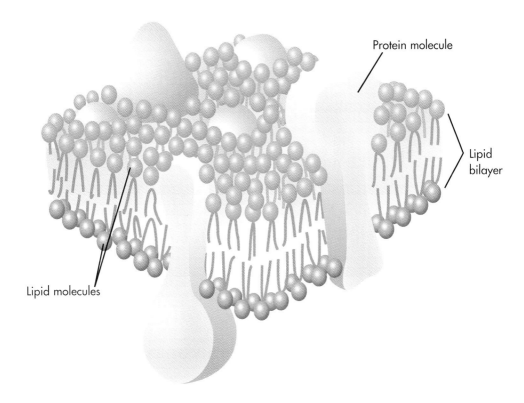

Protein molecule

Lipid bilayer

Lipid molecules

This diagram shows the basic components of a lipid bilayer, a semipermeable two-layer system that is arranged from millions of lipid molecules. The lipid "head" is hydrophilic ("water loving"), which means it attracts molecules. Its tail is hydrophobic ("water hating"), which means it repels molecules. This system protects the cell while at the same time allowing proteins to pass into and out of it.

The cell membrane is composed of lipid, protein, and carbohydrate molecules that are arranged in a flexible mosaic. The membrane's lipid molecules form two thin sheets, which are layered on top of each other. The two combined layers not only strengthen the cell wall but also act as a barrier to all but the very smallest molecules attempting to enter or leave the cell.

The proteins that pass through both lipid layers are often the ones involved in transporting signals across the membrane. Those that are positioned on the inside of the cell membrane may also be enzymes, capable of starting or changing an activity within the cell.

Proteins that sit outside the cell membrane are called receptors or "docking" proteins. These receptors watch and wait, on the lookout for certain molecules. Much like a lock and key, the receptors are looking for molecules with the right construction or fit. Docking proteins located in the membranes of intestinal cells are on the lookout for certain food molecules, which are absorbed and eventually relayed to the bloodstream.

Organelles

A semipermeable membrane also surrounds the cell's organelles. The function of the organelle membrane is similar to the cell membrane. It also contains receptors that regulate molecular movement across the membrane. These molecules often originate within the cell and are used as a form of communication between organelles.

Chapter Three

Cell Metabolism

The cellular process of producing and expending energy is known as metabolism. In order to function, all cells need energy. Without energy, no activities such as cell regulation can occur. A cell without an energy source is much like a car with an empty gas tank. Without the fuel, the car can't go anywhere. If a cell is without energy, it will soon die.

On Earth, the source of all energy for almost all life-forms is the Sun. Without the Sun, there would be no life. Through the process of photosynthesis, plants and algae are able to capture the Sun's rays and turn them into a food source and energy.

See the Light

Translated from Latin into English, the word "photosynthesis" actually means "constructing from light." In order for photosynthesis to occur in plant cells, several requirements must be met. In addition to sunlight, the plant must contain not only chlorophyll but also carbon dioxide and water. Chlorophyll is found within the chloroplasts, which are green-colored organelles. Carbon

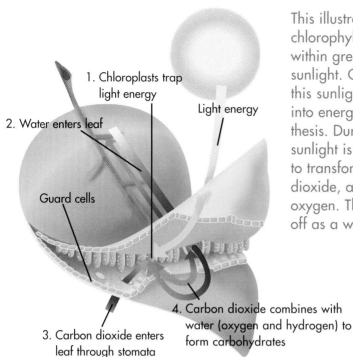

1. Chloroplasts trap light energy

Light energy

2. Water enters leaf

Guard cells

3. Carbon dioxide enters leaf through stomata

4. Carbon dioxide combines with water (oxygen and hydrogen) to form carbohydrates

This illustration shows how chlorophyll-containing cells within green leaves absorb sunlight. Once absorbed, this sunlight is transformed into energy during photosynthesis. During this process, sunlight is captured and used to transform water, carbon dioxide, and minerals into oxygen. This oxygen is given off as a waste product.

dioxide is a gas, and it enters the plant through openings called stomata on the surface of its leaves. The stomata are dominated by guard cells, which regulate movement of the gases into and out of the leaf. Water enters the plant through its roots.

The first step in this process occurs when a beam of sunlight hits the chlorophyll contained in the plant cell's chloroplasts. The protein molecules that make up the chlorophyll act as an energy trap. When the chlorophyll is hit by sunlight, bits of energy bounce off it and are grabbed by nearby carrier molecules.

The carrier molecules are able to use that energy to hitch together the carbon dioxide and water molecules into a variety of glucose, or sugar, molecules. Glucose is a carbohydrate. It is composed of carbon, hydrogen, and oxygen atoms. The bonds that hold those atoms together are also where the Sun's energy is stored.

One of the waste products of photosynthesis is oxygen, which humans and animals need to breathe. As carbon dioxide enters the plant through its leaves, oxygen is expelled. Through the process of photosynthesis, plants are able to make their own food.

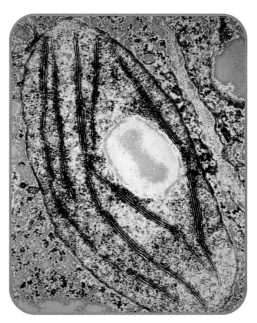

The chloroplast seen in this electron micrograph is from a pea plant. Chloroplasts are the sites of photosynthesis, the process by which plants obtain nutrients such as carbohydrates from carbon dioxide using the energy from sunlight.

Energy Makers and Takers

Green plants are called autotrophs because they manufacture their own energy. Animals, including humans, are called heterotrophs because they are unable to produce their own energy. They must "steal" energy either from plants or other animals.

Whether or not an organism can make its own energy, it must be able to break down that energy to use it. Both plant cells and animal cells must

Ancient Bacteria

Almost all cells can trace their energy source back to photosynthesis, but there are some notable exceptions. Biologists believe that the very first cells captured energy from the breakdown of chemicals such as hydrogen sulfide and methane. These cells are called archaebacteria, which means "ancient bacteria." Far from being extinct, this unique type of bacteria can be found in the superhot water that emanates from natural geysers.

harvest the energy stored in the chemical bonds of the food they take in, whether that food comes from a plant or another animal.

Again, the cell membrane plays a large role in regulating what food molecules are able to enter the cell. Throughout the cell membrane, there are glucose receptors. Composed of protein, they grab passing glucose molecules and pull them into the cell.

Glycolysis

The most common cell food is glucose. Even cells that are able to harvest energy from fats and amino acids (proteins) convert these fats and proteins to glucose. The process of making energy from glucose molecules is called glycolysis. Breaking down these molecules requires the cell to use ATP (adenosine triphosphate). ATP is a molecule found in all living organisms, and it is an energy source for cell functions. However, the energy the cell receives from breaking down the glucose molecule is far greater than the energy with which it begins the process. Not surprisingly, the steps involved in breaking down glucose are the opposite of the steps involved in creating it. Glucose plus oxygen is broken down to create carbon dioxide plus water and ATP.

Excess ATP not immediately used to drive cell functions is transferred to the cell's mitochondria for storage. The cell's ATP requirements vary according to its functions. For instance, muscle cells are filled with much more mitochondria and have much higher energy needs than skin cells do.

While all cells need energy in order to survive, each cell has limits on how much energy it can metabolize and store. When cell receptors detect that ATP levels are too high, for example, glucose will be converted to fat.

Chapter Four

Growth and Reproduction

One of the most important elements of a cell's existence is its ability to grow and reproduce itself. Cells reproduce for several reasons. If the organism is in a growth phase, more cells are needed as it increases in size. Cells also reproduce to replace worn-down cells or repair damaged ones.

The process of two cells dividing is called mitosis. During this process, one cell divides into two identical cells. Each new cell is called a daughter cell. Both daughter cells are identical to the parent cell.

In complex organisms, the body's cells are in a constant cycle of growth, reproduction, and death. As a cell grows older, its regulation mechanisms begin to break down and it no longer is able to receive critical messages upon which its survival depends.

Why Divide?

The cell's function dictates how often it will reproduce. Cells that line the intestinal tracks of animals die quickly because their environment is very hostile. Because of that, they have a short life span and reproduce more often.

With each cell, there are regulatory mechanisms that direct it when to divide and when not to divide. One of those mechanisms is called contact inhibition. When cells become so numerous that they begin to crowd each other, a chemical message that inhibits mitosis, or cell division, is sent from cell to cell.

When cells lack that mechanism, they are capable of endangering the survival of the organism. Cancer is an example of a disease in which cells have lost the feedback mechanism that limits reproduction.

There is much more to division than simply splitting the cell in half. In order for there to be two exact daughter cells, the parent cell must go through a series of phases before it can divide. At each step of mitosis, signals are being sent and received, each of which has a very distinct role in starting or stopping the various phases of mitosis.

Interphase

Before cell division can begin, the cell goes through a preliminary period called interphase. During this period, the cell expands in overall mass and all its organelles duplicate. Inside the nucleus, the chromosomes make copies of themselves. During interphase, each chromosome, composed of two coiled strands, begins to unwind, or unzip. As the strand unzips, enzymes travel up and down the two newly single

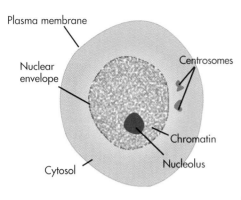

Plasma membrane

Nuclear envelope

Centrosomes

Chromatin

Nucleolus

Cytosol

strands and create one new copy of each.

At the end of interphase in a human cell, forty-six chromosomes have become ninety-two. In other words, two identical chromosome sets have been created from the original forty-six. To make sure that the daughter cells get half of a matched pair of chromosomes, the two sets of chromosomes stay joined together by a centromere. In this form, the chromosomes are called chromatids.

Phase I: Prophase

Mitosis, the division of both the nucleus and the cell, officially begins during prophase. Inside the nucleus, the chromatids begin to bunch up and form a line. The cell's two centrioles position themselves on either side of the nucleus, at right angles to the chromatids. Like a spider spinning a web, the two chromatids

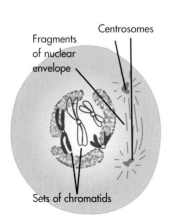

Fragments of nuclear envelope

Centrosomes

Sets of chromatids

shoot out fibrous spindles. The spindles meet mid-cell and form a football-shaped web around the nucleus.

At this point, if you looked at the cell under a microscope, you would notice that the nuclear membrane (also called the nuclear envelope) is starting to disappear. It's actually still there but broken down into small parts, which are stored in tiny little packets. Later, those packets will be used to build two brand-new nuclei.

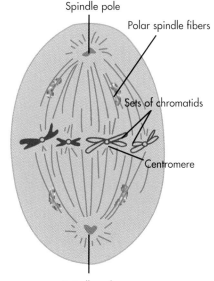

Spindle pole

Polar spindle fibers

Sets of chromatids

Centromere

Spindle pole

Phase II: Metaphase

During metaphase, the chromatids begin to attach themselves to the spindles springing from the centrioles. The centromeres, which hold the pairs together, line up along the middle of the cell, known as the equatorial plane. To get a visual, think of the equatorial plane as Earth's equator, with the centrioles positioned at the North and South Poles.

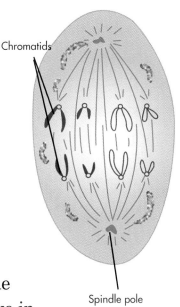

Chromatids

Spindle pole moving outward

Phase III: Anaphase

During anaphase, the centromeres that have held the paired chromatids divide. Each chromatid becomes a separate chromosome. Using the centriole spindles to guide them, the once-attached chromosomes move in opposite directions—one heading toward the "top" part of the cell and the other toward the "bottom."

Phase IV: Telophase

During telophase, the cell itself is still whole, but it has become pinched at the middle. Inside the cell,

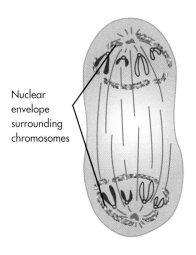

Nuclear envelope surrounding chromosomes

there are two of everything, but each set of organelles is crowded on opposite sides of the cell. During telophase, the spindles fade away and the nuclear membrane that was packed away reemerges and forms two new nuclei. The bunched-up chromosomes relax and expand back into thin, wavy strands.

Phase V: Cytokinesis

During cytokinesis, the one cell becomes two daughter cells. In this phase, the membrane that surrounds the cell begins to move inward on itself. Think of slowly tightening a rope wrapped around a water balloon, and you have the picture. In animals, the

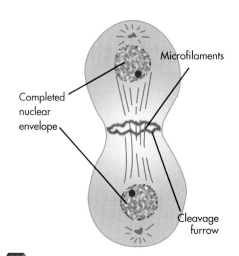

Microfilaments

Completed nuclear envelope

Cleavage furrow

Variation on a Theme

Although both plant cells and animal cells go through the process of cell division, there are some minor differences for each type. For example, plant cells don't have centrioles, but spindles do form during mitosis. Another difference results from the thickness of animal cells versus plant cells. Plant cell walls are thicker and stiffer than animal cell membranes. Because of that, the plant cell can't use the pinch process to separate. Instead, batches of carbohydrates line up along the equatorial plane of the cell. Eventually, they form a new cell wall that separates the two cells completely.

new wall is called a cleavage furrow, and in plants, it is called a cell plate. Eventually, the cell pinches into two identical parts.

The Great Unknown

Through careful observation and improved technology, biologists have been able to explain the details of mitosis in detail. Still, when it comes to the exact processes that trigger and control the different phases of mitosis, there is still much research to be done. And while new discoveries are being made all the time, the mystery of life still holds many riddles.

Chapter Five

One Plus One Equals One

In addition to growth and repair, an organism's survival depends on its ability to reproduce. We all know, after all, that dogs don't "sprout" puppies, and while it might make for good science fiction, humans don't either.

At some point during our evolutionary history, Mother Nature discovered that although asexual reproduction had its advantages, it also had its limitations. If two organisms could somehow come together and exchange genetic information, the next generation of organisms would contain a much more varied genetic mix. In nature, life-forms are made stronger when they are able to adapt to a changing environment. Sexual reproduction ensures a greater variety of genes from which to choose. These choices result in greater genetic variability.

The idea was a good one, but there was a slight complication. If two organisms combined their chromosomes, the resulting offspring would have double the chromosomes of the parent. Nature's big trick was to create specialized cells designed specifically for sexual reproduction. Those specialized cells would have exactly half the number of chromosomes as cells in the rest of the organism's body.

Sex Cells

The cells involved in sexual reproduction are called germ cells. They are created in the organism's gonads (or the archegonium in plants). When the organism reaches maturity, the germ cells form sex cells through the process of meiosis.

The sex cells of a female are called eggs, or ova. The sex cells of a male are called sperm. When an ovum joins with the sperm, fertilization occurs. The combined cell is called a zygote, and it has the potential to develop into a new life.

Meiosis and mitosis have a lot in common. In addition to sounding alike, they also share similar

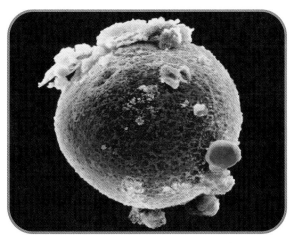 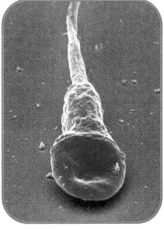

This scanning electron micrograph *(left)* shows a single human ovum (egg) after it has been fertilized by a human sperm cell. On the right is a similar micrograph of the head of a human sperm cell, which is produced in the male testes. Its rounded head contains the male hereditary material (DNA), and it is propelled by a single flagellum.

phases. Also, while researchers know all the steps involved in meiosis as they do with mitosis, they are still in the beginning phases of understanding what regulates its different phases.

One of the differences between meiosis and mitosis is that in mitosis, there is a single cell division. Meiosis involves two divisions, which produce four daughter cells. The two divisions are called meiosis I and meiosis II. Unlike mitosis, each of those four cells has only half the chromosomes of the original cell.

Meiosis I begins with interphase I. It is followed by prophase I, metaphase I, anaphase I, telophase I, and finally cytokinesis, when one cell divides and becomes two. In animal cells, a cleavage furrow forms and the cells literally pinch apart. (Plants form a cell plate, which doesn't pinch as much as it forms a new wall.)

Phase II of meiosis then begins. Unlike mitosis, the purpose of meiosis is not to make duplicate cells. It is to create specialized sex cells in order to form a new and genetically unique organism.

Meiosis II consists of almost all the same phases as meiosis I. The phases are prophase II, metaphase II, anaphase II, telophase II, and cytokinesis. What's missing is interphase. The chromosomes of the daughter cells are not copied again, so when the process is complete, the result will be four haploid cells. These cells are called haploid cells because each one has half the chromosomes of the original cell.

Meiosis II

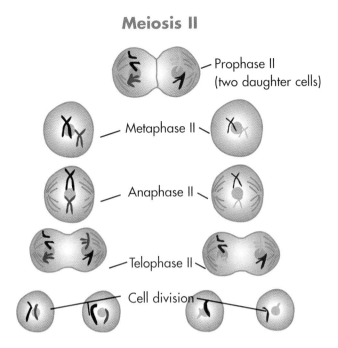

Prophase II
(two daughter cells)

Metaphase II

Anaphase II

Telophase II

Cell division

The second division of meiosis is shown in this illustration. During meiosis II, each haploid daughter cell divides, and each chromatid pair divides into two separate chromosomes. These chromosomes are then pulled to the opposite ends of the daughter cells. In the end of the process, each daughter cell divides again, producing four haploid gametes, or mature cells.

In the case of male animals, the four haploid cells are better known as sperm. Each microscopic sperm has a whiplike "tail" called a flagellum that enables it to move. In female animals, one of the four haploid cells results in an egg, or ovum.

During meiosis in a human, one of the haploid cells essentially "steals" all the cytoplasm from the original cell. Once a sperm fertilizes the egg, it needs all that cytoplasm to feed the newly formed organism. The three other smaller cells are called polar bodies, and they eventually break down and disappear.

Chapter Six

Multiply and Specialize

The development of a new organism begins when a sperm cell makes contact with the surface of an egg during fertilization. The nuclei of the egg and the sperm move to the center of the egg cell. They fuse together to form the nucleus of the zygote, the name of the single cell formed by the union of a single sperm and an egg.

That zygote has the potential to transform itself into a highly complex organism. Depending on the organism, it may include billions of specialized cells. Once the zygote begins to divide, it is called an embryo. The name of the science that studies this transformation is called embryology.

Embryology is a young science. It began just over a century ago. Until then, most scientists thought that sperm contained miniature versions of adult organisms. The idea was that through sexual intercourse, a teeny-tiny animal was planted in the female's body where it would grow and expand until it was ready to be born. Even after the invention of the microscope many years ago, there were some researchers who said they could see miniature children curled up in human sperm cells!

Today, we know that a fetus actually begins as a single cell, the zygote. Each zygote contains a complete set of chromosomes unique to that zygote. Those chromosomes are very much like a blueprint, a plan the cell will constantly refer back to as it divides and grows.

Each time the zygote divides, its set of original blueprints is exactly copied and passed on to each daughter cell. As a result, each organism's cells contain a complete blueprint to build a whole new organism. For example, although a muscle cell might not need or use genetic information related to skin cell formation, it's all right there in the muscle cell's nucleus.

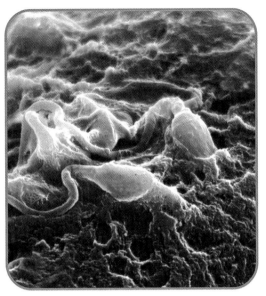

In this colored electron micrograph, two human sperm cells *(orange)* attempt to fertilize a human ovum *(egg, blue)*. While women usually produce one egg each month for fertilization, males may release as many as 300 million sperm cells during sexual intercourse. Of the millions of sperm cells, however, only a few hundred compete to penetrate the egg's wall, and only one will fuse with its nucleus. Once the fertilization has begun, the female's egg cell forms a barrier against other sperm cells.

The key to the development of specialized cells is contained in the genes. The genes produce special proteins, which regulate what portion of its genetic blueprint it will express.

The Cell Next Door

Cell differentiation and regulation occur as soon as the single-celled zygote divides for the first time. Within the embryo, the cells don't exist independently of each other. Cells in multicellular organisms are in constant communication with each other. They send chemical messages that pass through one membrane to another. These messages have the power to transform both the appearance and roles of other cells.

The messages also play a big role in cell differentiation. One cell, for example, might tell its neighbor to focus on making a particular type of protein. When that cell divides, the daughter cells also make that protein and then signal their neighbors to make more of it. This process is called induction, and it plays a very important role in the early states of embryonic development.

One example of induction can be observed early on in an embryo's development. On the sixth day after fertilization, the embryo is made up of about 120 cells. Through the process of induction, groups of cells join together to make enzymes, which will help situate the embryo in the uterine wall, located in the female's reproductive organs.

Animal Embryology

Scientists divide embryonic development into three different stages. The states are cleavage, gastrulation, and organogenesis.

Cleavage

Cleavage officially begins when the zygote starts to divide. Although there are a number of divisions during this phase, the embryo doesn't increase in size. This is because the cells skip over the normal growth phase between divisions. Each time there is a division, the daughter cells decrease in size.

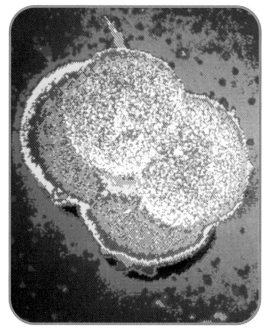

This computer-enhanced scanning electron micrograph shows two views of cell cleavage (division) during early animal embryo development.

As this point, the cell is still the same size as the original zygote. The place where those two balls are pressed up against each other is where the embryo will form. One ball is the yolk sac (loaded with protein that provides nutrition to organisms that grow in eggs). The other ball will eventually become the amniotic sac, a fluid-filled "bag" that protects the growing organism from bumps and jolts throughout its development.

Gastrulation

During gastrulation, the ball of cells is transformed into a multilayered organism with recognizable cell differentiation. In humans, this occurs about two weeks after fertilization. While this phase may occur at different times in different organisms, the movement and organization of cells is remarkably similar.

The most important activity is the transformation of cells into the beginnings of the embryo. The embryo will have three distinct layers: the external ectoderm, the internal endoderm, and the intermediate mesoderm.

The cells that line the inside of the embryo are called the endoderm. Those cells will eventually become the animal's digestive tract, as well as other internal organs. The cells layered on the outside of the embryo will become the organism's ectoderm, including the skin, nervous system, and parts of the eye and inner ear. The third layer, located between the endoderm and ectoderm, is the mesoderm. "Meso" in "mesoderm" means "middle," and it is in this layer that the heart, muscles, bones, blood, and sex organs will develop.

Scientists are still in the beginning stages of trying to understand what guides cell movement during this phase. Currently, there is evidence that the movement is directed by genetic signals. These signals can either cause cells to stick together or promote movement.

Organ Formation

With the three layers in place as a foundation, the embryo can begin building actual organs. This process is called organogenesis. As the embryo cells divide, the daughter cells assume forms and functions different from those of the mother cell. In some cases, the two daughter cells will head in completely different directions, forming different tissues or organs.

Some cells may be programmed to function for a short period but then self-destruct. This process is called programmed cell death. Human embryos—like all embryos with a backbone, or spine, start out with tails and webbed hands and feet. Six weeks into development, those cells are sent "death" signals, which cause the cells to die.

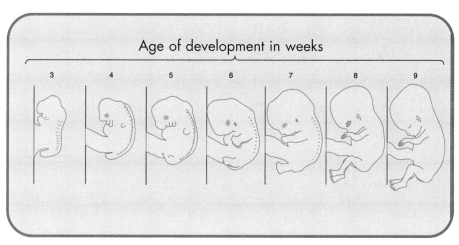

These illustrations document the development of a human embryo from the third week of development until nine weeks. At the end of the third week, a process known as gastrulation occurs, which means that three types of tissue (endoderm, mesoderm, and ectoderm) are formed. These tissues are known as germ layers. Between the third and eighth week, these tissues develop further into the body's nervous, respiratory, and vascular systems, gastrointestinal tract, skin, kidneys, and other organs. By the ninth week, the fetus has limbs, digits, and a humanlike face.

The yolk of the fertilized egg fuels this process for most animals. Mammal growth is more complex and requires more energy than the yolk can provide. Early in its development, the embryo plants itself in the mother's uterine wall. There, the embryo forms a direct connection with the mother's blood supply, from which it can receive essential nutrients.

A Shared Past

One of the most fascinating aspects of embryology occurs during early development. About four weeks after fertilization, vertebrate animal embryos possess a clearly defined head and the beginnings of arm and leg "buds." These will later develop into limbs. What's amazing is that it is almost impossible to tell the difference between various animal embryos.

A four-week-old human embryo looks very much like a cat or leopard or hawk embryo. All of them have not only tails but also gill pouches, which will develop into gills in fish. In humans, the tail will shrink and those gills will develop into parts of the human face.

This similarity hints at the evolutionary links between all life-forms. It also points out that while genetic information might not be finally expressed, it's still there lurking in the background. In a fish embryo, the genes that control gill development can still be triggered. Scientists think that in humans, those genes are either absent, inactive, or have evolved into something else.

Plant Embryology

Like animals, many plants reproduce by the coming together of an egg and a sperm. When the plant zygote forms, it triggers cell division and development of the embryo. A seed is very much like an egg. Inside, it contains an embryo, which has the potential to grow into a plant.

The process of plant embryology is similar to animal embryology, but there are distinct differences between them. Plants have different systems, and scientists use different terminology to explain their reproductive process. For example, plant embryos are not born, they "germinate" from a seed.

Growth is another big difference between plants and animals. At some point, animals mature and stop growing. Certain parts of plants, however, remain in the embryonic phase. Even after it has reached a mature size, a plant's roots and shoots continue to grow throughout its life.

Exploring the Blueprint

Scientists have conducted experiments proving that cells are packed full of genetic memories. In one experiment, researchers transplanted some pancreatic cells into the brain. After the transplant, the cells "remembered" that they were pancreatic cells. They continued to make pancreatic hormones.

However, the experiment also showed that cells can be influenced by their environment. When those same pancreatic cells were placed in a test tube outside of the body, they behaved differently. Away from the organism, they forget their specialty. Many of them reverted to the blob shape and behavior of the single-celled amoeba. When the cells were placed back in their proper environment, their memory kicked in and they resumed their old functions.

Still, while environment can have a big effect on a cell's behavior, genes are still king. As the organism develops and cells specialize, certain genes in those cells are turned on, while others are permanently switched off. So while that pancreatic cell could survive as a simpler form, it lost the ability to differentiate.

Embryonic cells are fascinating entities. They appear to be incredibly simple, and yet they hold the key to our past, present, and future. As soon as the zygote forms, that one small cell contains all the information needed to create a complex, multicelled organism. Although scientists have a long way to go before they have a complete understanding of how cells are reproduced and regulated, we are well on our way to comprehending these complex biological processes.

Glossary

anaphase (A-nuh-fayz) Phase of cell division when the paired chromosomes separate and move to opposite ends of the dividing cell.

centriole (SEN-tree-ohl) One of a pair of organelles that creates spindles, which assist in chromosomal division.

centromere (SEN-troh-meer) A specialized part of the chromosome region to which spindle fibers attach during cell division.

chromatid (KROH-muh-tid) One-half of a replicated chromosome.

chromosome (KROH-muh-sohm) A cell structure made of DNA, which contains all of the cell's genetic information in the form of genes.

cleavage (KLEE-vij) A series of early cell divisions of the fertilized ovum.

cytokinesis (sy-toh-kin-EE-sis) Division of the cytoplasm producing two distinct daughter cells.

differentiation (dif-uh-ren-shee-AY-shun) The process by which an undifferentiated embryonic cell becomes a specialized cell, such as a heart, liver, or muscle cell.

DNA (deoxyribonucleic acid) (dee-AHK-see-ry-boh-noo-klay-ik A-sid) A chemical that makes up chromosomes. DNA directs how an organism will develop and mature.

ectoderm (EK-toh-derm) The outermost layer of a group of cells, which will eventually develop into the skin, nervous system, and parts of the eye and inner ear.

embryo (EM-bree-oh) The developing organism produced through sexual reproduction.

embryology (em-bree-AH-luh-jee) The study of the growth and development of the embryo.

endoderm (EN-doh-derm) The middle layer of a group of cells, which will eventually develop into the internal organs.

gastrulation (gas-troo-LAY-shun) The process by which a fertilized egg becomes a multilayered embryo.

induction (in-DUK-shun) The process by which one cell or a set of cells influences the behavior of another cell or cells.

interphase (IN-tur-fayz) The phase of cell division when cell organelles and chromosomes duplicate.

meiosis (my-OH-sis) A two-part (meiosis I and meiosis II) cell division process by which organisms sexually reproduce.

mesoderm (MEH-so-derm) The middle layer of a group of cells, which eventually develops into the heart, muscles, bones, blood, and sex organs.

metaphase (MEH-tuh-fayz) The phase of cell division when chromosomes align.

mitosis (my-TOH-sis) A form of cell division in which a cell divides and produces two daughter cells from a single parent cell.

nuclear membrane (NOO-klee-ur MEM-brayn) A membrane that separates the contents of the nucleus from the cytoplasm.

nucleus (NOO-klee-us) A membrane-bound structure that contains the cell's hereditary information and controls the cell's growth and reproduction.

organogenesis (or-gan-oh-JEN-uh-sis) A phase during cellular development when the embryo develops internal organs.

ovum (OH-vum) A female sex cell, also known as the egg, produced by the female for sexual reproduction.

prophase (PRO-fayz) During this phase of cell division, the chromosomes and spindles form between the cell's two centrioles.

ribosome (RY-buh-sohm) A protein-producing organelle located in the cytoplasm of a living cell.

RNA (ribonucleic acid) (ry-boh-noo-KLAY-ik A-sid)
Genetic material found in the nucleus and cytoplasm of a cell. It converts genetic information from DNA to proteins. There are three different types of RNA.

telophase (TEL-uh-fayz) The phase of cell division when the nucleus of one cell is divided equally into two nuclei.

zygote (ZY-goht) The cell formed by the union of the egg and sperm.

For More Information

Cell Magazine
1100 Massachusetts Avenue
Cambridge, MA 02138
(617) 661-7057

Discover Magazine
114 Fifth Avenue
New York, NY 10011
(212) 633-4400
Web site: http://discover.com

Web Sites

Due to the changing nature of Internet links, the Rosen Publishing Group, Inc., has developed an online list of Web sites related to the subject of this book. This site is updated regularly. Please use this link to access the list:

http://www.rosenlinks.com/lce/cere

For Further Reading

Nicolov, Nicolay, and Orlin Ivanov. *Cells & Cell Division.* Philadelphia: Coronet Books, 2002.

Snedden, Robert. *Cell Division & Genetics.* Oxford, England: Heinemann Library, 2002.

Bibliography

Fritz, Sandy. *Understanding Cloning.* Victoria, Australia: Warner Books, 2002.

Jones, Steve. *The Language of Genes.* New York: Doubleday, 1993.

Nicholl, Desmond S. *An Introduction to Genetic Engineering.* Cambridge, MA: Cambridge University Press, 2002.

Prentice, David A., and Michael A. Palladino. *Stem Cells and Cloning.* San Francisco: Benjamin-Cummings Publishing Company, 2002.

Prentice Hall Science editors. *Cells: Building Blocks of Life.* Englewood Cliffs, NJ: Prentice Hall, 1994.

Rensberger, Boyce. *Life Itself.* New York: Oxford University Press, 1996.

Silverstein, Alvin. *Cells.* Brookfield, CT: Twenty-First Century Books, 2002.

Sperelakis, Nicholas. *Cell Physiology Source Book.* San Diego: Academic Press, 1998.

Thomas, Lewis. *The Lives of a Cell.* New York: The Viking Press, 1974.

Index

About the Author

Lois Sakany is a freelance author who lives in New York City.

Credits

Cover, p. 1 © John Durham/Science Photo Library; pp. 6, 7, 8, 11, 14, 15, 17, 20, 26, 27, 28, 33 by Tahara Anderson; pp. 10, 21 © Dr. Jeremy Burgess/Science Photo Library; p. 31 (left) © Motta & Familiari/Anatomy Department/University "La Sapienza," Rome/Science Photo Library; p. 31 (right) © VVG/Science Photo Library; p. 35 © Pascal Goetgheluck/ Science Photo Library; p. 37 © Dr. Gerard Schatten/Science Photo Library; p. 39 © Peter Gardiner/Science Photo Library.

Designer: Tahara Anderson; **Editor:** Joann Jovinelly